On the Job

FREDERICK KOH

Editorial Board
David Booth • Joan Green • Jack Booth

STECK-VAUGHN
Harcourt Achieve

www.HarcourtAchieve.com

10801 N. Mopac Expressway
Building # 3
Austin, TX 78759
1.800.531.5015

Steck-Vaughn is a trademark of Harcourt Achieve Inc. registered in the
United States of America and/or other jurisdictions. All inquiries should
be mailed to Harcourt Achieve Inc., P.O. Box 27010, Austin, TX 78755.

Ru'bicon © 2006 Rubicon Publishing Inc.
www.rubiconpublishing.com

Project Editors: Miriam Bardswich, Kim Koh
Editor: Sarah Symonds
Editorial Assistant: Caitlin Drake
Creative Director: Jennifer Drew-Tremblay
Art Director: Jen Harvey
Designer: Deanna Bishop

6 7 8 9 10   5 4 3 2 1

On the Job
ISBN 1-4190-2466-3

CONTENTS

4   **Introduction**

6   **Celebrities' Early Jobs**
Maintenance worker, telemarketer, Cheerio-dust sweeper … In this series of profiles, find out what your favorite celebrities did *before* they became famous.

10   **A Gig in the Great Outdoors**
A newspaper article about a man who flies over the gorgeous scenery of a provincial park for a living.

12   **Woman at Work**
Profile of a woman who has risen to the top of her field in one of today's most popular trades.

14   **Behind the Scenes**
What does a scenic carpenter have to do with the movie industry? You'll find out in this interview.

18   **Growing Up**
This father isn't mean; he's just had enough. Read how his decision plays out in this graphic story.

22   **Changing Image**
Dealing with medical emergencies, enforcing the law, helping passengers evacuate to safety … In this news article, you'll learn that flight attendants do a lot more than serve food in the sky.

26   **Cushy Jobs in Sports**
All-star athletes get paid big bucks to perform well for their teams, but what about the bench-warmers? Get the scoop in this newspaper article.

32   **The Professional**
According to this personal account, anyone can be a professional — regardless of the job title.

36   **Get Me Some Poets as Managers**
This article tracks the increasing need for creativity in the professional world. Check it out.

39   **The Interview**
This interview experience is not what you would expect. Read this poem to find out what happens.

40   **Dear Alex …**
When in doubt about your job, seek advice; better still, read this advice column.

42   **Crime in the Workplace**
Follow this script and solve the mystery of the strange disappearance of a shipment of computer chips.

CHOOSE A JOB YOU LOVE, AND YOU'LL NEVER HAVE TO WORK A DAY IN YOUR LIFE.

– Confucius

Celebrities

Jennifer Aniston

Known best for her role as Rachel Green on the hit sitcom *Friends*, Jennifer Aniston has been the center of media attention for over a decade. Her show was a success, her hairstyle became a phenomenon, and now she's a much sought-after actress. Her movie career is on the rise with roles in successful movies like *Along Came Polly* and *Bruce Almighty*. Aniston has won an Emmy and a number of People's Choice Awards for her work on *Friends*.

Now an actor, once a waitress.

Michael Jordan

Michael Jordan is among the best-known athletes in the world, and many argue that he is the best basketball player to ever show his skills on the court. He was a leading scorer in the NBA and led his team, the Chicago Bulls, to many championships. Jordan also played baseball with the Chicago White Sox before returning to basketball to finish his career.

Now a basketball player, once a hotel maintenance worker.

Early Jobs

Stephen King is a prolific American author best known for his horror novels. He creeps out many who dare to read his books late at night. Stephen King's first published novel was *Carrie* (1974). Many of his books, both fiction and nonfiction, are top sellers and some have been adapted for movies.

Now an author, once an industrial laundry worker.

prolific: *productive*

Ashton Kutcher

Ashton Kutcher is one of the hottest actors in Hollywood. He's best known for his role as Michael Kelso in *That '70s Show*. He's loved by his fans but feared by many celebrities; they do not want to be the target of one of Kutcher's pranks on his show *Punk'd*. Ashton has proved his popularity by winning the most Teen Choice Awards in the show's history.

Now an actor, once a Cheerio-dust sweeper.

J.K. Rowling

J.K. Rowling was a little-known fiction writer who achieved fame and international attention when her novel *Harry Potter and the Sorcerer's Stone* was published in 1997. The fortune from her Harry Potter movies and book rights is estimated by *Forbes* magazine at $1 billion, making her the first billionaire from writing books. What an achievement for a single parent who was struggling to make ends meet barely a few years back.

Now a fiction writer, once a secretary.

Angela Ruggiero

Angela Ruggiero is a star member of the U.S. National Women's Hockey Team. In the last two winter Olympics, Ruggiero's team won the gold and silver medals. She was the first female non–goalie to ever play in the CHL. Ruggiero was named the best female college hockey player in her senior year at Harvard and was rated the number one female hockey player in the world by *The Hockey News* in 2004.

Now a hockey player, once a real estate broker.

CHL: *Central Hockey League*

Angela Ruggiero: (left)

Gwen Stefani

Gwen Stefani was the lead singer for the band *No Doubt* before going solo in 2004 with her first album, *Love. Angel. Music. Baby*. Stefani has been known for her unique and funky style, so the arrival of her L.A.M.B. clothing line came as no surprise to her fans. Stefani made her acting debut in the movie *The Aviator,* where she played screen legend Jean Harlow.

Now a singer/songwriter/clothing designer, once a Dairy Queen floor scrubber.

Kanye West

Kanye West spent his early days producing songs for big hip-hop artists like Jay-Z before he launched his own rapping career. West was thrust into the spotlight with the arrival of his first album, *The College Dropout*, in 2004. West uses sample hooks and trademark rhythms in his music. He is on a short path to success, having already won multiple Grammys for his first album.

Now a singer/songwriter, once a telemarketer.

Owen Wilson

Owen Wilson is a comedic actor known for his great improvisation skills. He's co-written many of the screenplays for movies in which he has appeared. Wilson has a distinctive-looking nose, which was broken when he was playing football in high school. Owen has been in many popular comedies, including *Meet the Parents*, *Wedding Crashers,* and *Starsky & Hutch*.

Now an actor, once a pool cleaner.

improvisation: *not scripted, spontaneous*

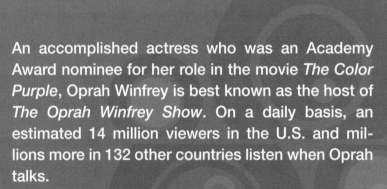

Oprah Winfrey

An accomplished actress who was an Academy Award nominee for her role in the movie *The Color Purple*, Oprah Winfrey is best known as the host of *The Oprah Winfrey Show*. On a daily basis, an estimated 14 million viewers in the U.S. and millions more in 132 other countries listen when Oprah talks.

Now a talk show host, once a news reader.

wrap up

1. Imagine you have a chance to interview one of the celebrities. Who would you choose and what would you like to know? Write a list of interview questions to ask the celebrity.

2. Create a help-wanted ad for one of these celebrities' early jobs. Be sure to include the type of person the company is looking for.

WEB CONNECTIONS

Search the Internet for another two celebrities to add to the list. Follow the same format — provide a short description of the celebrity, and mention his or her early job.

A Gig in the Great Outdoors

Hudson wouldn't trade his job "for anything"

From *Metro*, July 4, 2005

warm up

Think of jobs in the great outdoors. Is that somewhere you would like to work? Why or why not?

Imagine waking up for work every morning — yawn, stretch — in a lakeside cottage in Algonquin Park.

Your "office" is just a short walk away, floating on two pontoons at the dock. It's a de Havilland DHC-2 MK III, also known as a Turbo Beaver. And a typical workday will involve flying some very interesting people over some of the most beautiful terrain in the province.

Not bad, eh? "I wouldn't trade it for anything," says Jim Hudson with a boyish grin.

CHECKPOINT

What is Jim Hudson's job?

Under contract to the forest fire management program of the Ministry of Natural Resources, the 39-year-old is the current pilot of the park. If you've been camping or canoeing in Algonquin, you've very likely seen the brilliant yellow and black (the ministry's signature aircraft colors) craft buzzing overhead or coming in for a landing on water.

If you've been injured or lost in the park's interior, you might have felt immense relief at the sight of this workhorse. And if you've been poaching, it's likely the last thing you'd want to see heading in your direction.

Jim Hudson spends much of his time puddle jumping from lake to lake in the southern section of Algonquin Park. He pilots a Turbo Beaver aircraft and does everything from tracking wolves by telemetry to delivering park rangers into the interior.

pontoons: *floats*
poaching: *catching animals illegally*
telemetry: *transmission of data by radio from remote sources*

"People either love to see this yellow bird come or they hate to see it come. It depends on the circumstances," says Hudson, who's been a bush pilot for 18 years and has logged more than 11,000 hours behind the props of aircraft like Turbo Beavers and Otters. ...

props: *propellers*

FYI

The Turbo Beaver is known to be reliable, sturdy, and safe. It is still widely used by bush pilots and park pilots in North America and all over the world.

wrap up

1. What does it say about Hudson's job that he "wouldn't trade it for anything"? In the voice of Jim Hudson, describe what a typical day on the job is like.

2. Imagine you are Jim Hudson speaking to an audience about your job. Highlight your responsibilities, and describe the qualifications, training, and personal qualities that you bring to the job.

WEB CONNECTIONS

Using the Internet, look up one of the U.S. national parks. Create a poster to attract people to the park. Describe the activities for each season and include a map to show the location.

WOMAN AT WORK

Construction jobs offer great pay and are always in demand. Every year, hundreds of thousands of new hires are needed just to keep up with the demand for roads, homes, schools, airports, office buildings, industrial plants, and more!

CHECKPOINT

What do you know about apprenticeship programs? Share your information with a partner.

Many people start in the trades by enrolling in apprenticeship programs, which are offered through trade associations, unions, vocational schools, and community colleges. Apprenticeships typically last four years, but can vary from two to five years, depending on the field and the state. Another way is to learn skills on the job. This less formal training can be a great learning experience.

The industry offers a choice of careers — from skilled trades, construction supervision, project management, marketing, and teaching to design and engineering. It's always a good idea to talk to someone in the field to get more information.

warm up

In a small group, brainstorm images, slogans, and a brief message for a poster about the construction industry. Keep in mind your audience is young adults.

Profile

Name: Ann Schuessler
Job: Superintendent in a construction company
Age: 34
Education: B.A. Real Estate Finance, Indiana University

CHECKPOINT

What do you think Ann means by this?

On construction industry opportunities: "With the labor shortage, now is a great time for women, or anyone, to get work in construction. But even in bad times, if you do your work well, you're going to get opportunities. Companies value dependable, good workers."

On being a woman in a non-traditional field: "I don't like separation, as in 'here are all the men, and over here are all the women.' I try not to differentiate between the guys and myself because I want [gender] to be a non-issue. The best way to overcome stereotypes is to just do your job well, then people realize that it isn't a big deal."

Ann's tips for women in the trades:

- Have a good sense of humor. Don't sweat the little stuff, and don't get hung up on every small problem. Instead, keep focused on your job, and do it well.

- Be proactive in pursuing goals. No one is going to hold your hand during your career; but at the same time, most people won't stand in your way if you take the initiative toward your own goals.

- Get a variety of experiences. I began my professional career as a project engineer in the field, and also worked as a carpenter between jobs. I varied my job titles to get the experience needed to manage an entire project.

- Do a good job. Even if some people on the job have old-fashioned attitudes toward women in the construction industry, no one can argue with a job well done. Basically, people want to work with others who get the job done right, male or female.

stereotypes: *preconceived ideas about someone or something*
proactive: *hands-on*

wrap up

1. In your own words, describe how Ann deals with the gender issue in her workplace.

2. Imagine you have a chance to interview Ann. Write down five questions to ask her about her job.

WEB CONNECTIONS

Would you choose the construction field? Why or why not? Use the Internet to research jobs in the construction industry, such as design and engineering, construction management, and skilled trades.

Behind the Scenes

warm up

What jobs come to mind when you think about the motion picture industry? Which of these jobs take place behind the scenes?

Rob Nason majored in Economics and started off with an office job. Today he is a scenic carpenter in the film industry and millions see his work. What exactly does he do? BOLDPRINT interviews Rob Nason to find out.

BOLDPRINT: What is a scenic carpenter?

ROB NASON: Unlike a regular carpenter who works with wood to build furniture for everyday use, a scenic carpenter creates settings and props to simulate real live scenes for a film. The scene could be a modern office one day and an 18th century saloon the next day. On another day, I could be building a spaceship, a dinosaur, a theme park, or even a museum display. It's never the same thing.

BP: What kinds of films have you worked on?

RN: I have worked on many television productions, such as *Nikita, Mutant X, Queer as Folk, The Hardy Boys,* and *The Pete Rose Story*, as well as many movies of the week.

BP: Do you have the opportunity to meet celebrities on your job?

RN: As scenic carpenters, we don't have very much interaction with celebrities but we do see them when we are on set. I have met Peta Wilson, who starred in *Nikita*, as well as Lou Diamond Phillips, Tiffani-Amber Thiessen, Jennie Garth, and Harvey Keitel, among others.

BP: What is a typical day for you like?

RN: Generally, it would start with my call

CHECKPOINT

As you read, note the skills involved in being a scenic carpenter.

simulate: *reproduce, imitate*

14

time at the shop at 7:00 AM. I would see the Head Carpenter to find out what jobs he is handing out. We would then go over drawings and discuss a plan on how my part of the job should be completed. From that point on, the workday is rarely typical. No two scenes or props are the same. I have to figure out the best approach, find the materials, improvise ways to circumvent problems, and still stay focused on doing the job right and on time!

BP: Do you use any special tools and materials in your work?

RN: I use pretty much every woodworking tool you can think of — all kinds of saws, planers, jointers, drill presses, screw guns, and staplers. As a scenic carpenter, I not only work with wood but also with paper, fabric, steel, acrylic sheeting, and plastic tubes. I often use different materials to fake a real scene or object.

BP: What skills are needed to get a job as a scenic carpenter?

RN: You would need to have the skills of a carpenter or a cabinetmaker, or have enough hours of apprenticeship in the trade to be able to hold your own. You have to understand the scenic world, the ability to imagine how things appear on camera, and to improvise ways to build them quickly and differently. Scenic carpenters have to be creative to be proficient at the job. For example, from an artist's drawing, you have to figure out what materials to use and how to achieve it. We have to make things appear real. It is important to think outside the box, know what you can get away with, and what you can't.

CHECKPOINT

What does "think outside the box" mean?

improvise: *construct with what is available*
circumvent: *avoid*

BP: How does one get into the trade? What are the necessary qualifications?

RN: It is important to get the right training. Find a company that is willing to train you or choose a good apprenticeship program. Apprenticeships offer classroom instruction and on-the-job training. They are a great way to pick up the skills. It takes about five years to become a qualified journey person, meaning a skilled worker.

BP: When and how did you get started?

RN: I didn't start off as a carpenter. I worked for a special events company and as a merchandiser before I tried out work with a scenic construction company. I told the manager I had experience in making props, which was a little of what I did when I worked at special events planning.

What I saw on my first day at work were work benches, lots of woodworking equipment and tools, and people moving at what seemed like 90 miles an hour. I knew I was way over my head.

CHECKPOINT

Why does Rob say this?

I had never used a table saw or seen a radial arm saw before. At the end of the day, the owner told me I was "green" (inexperienced). No kidding! He then told me he liked my attitude and that I could stay on to take care of the maintenance of the shop — run around and pick up supplies and help the carpenters when they needed a hand. I stayed with that company for two and a half years, and I learned a lot.

To answer your question, I didn't choose carpentry — it chose me. But I found carpentry to be a lot of fun and very rewarding. I had the satisfaction of seeing things that I had built and knowing that many others would have seen them too.

BP: So what did you do after you left that job?

RN: I joined a company that was doing the television show *Nikita* for Warner Brothers. I worked with one of the best crews in town. It was hard to keep up with the team, but my skills and knowledge of building scenic pieces took a quantum leap.

quantum leap: *sudden major change*

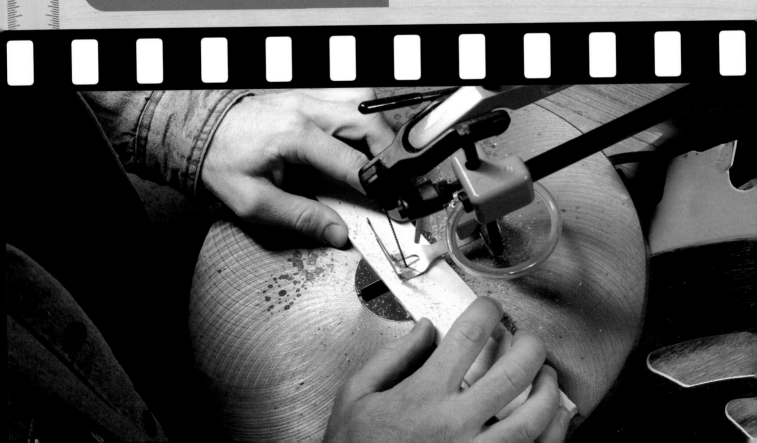

BP: What subjects in school are relevant to this trade?

RN: I think math is important — especially geometry. I also strongly recommend extracurricular activities in school, such as getting involved in clubs or team sports. It is important to be able to work well with others in this trade.

BP: What advice would you give to someone who is interested in your kind of work?

RN: I would say go for it, especially if you are physically strong and like doing things with your hands. It is hard work, but it is creative and very satisfying.

BP: What are some important attributes that contribute to your success?

RN: My work ethic is probably one of my most important attributes. I care about what I do and I set a very high standard for my work. I like people and I work well with others. Working on a film set is a team effort. You are always helping others complete their jobs and they are helping you too.

wrap up

1. Imagine you are the interviewer. Write a thank-you letter to Rob. Describe what you have learned about him and his job from the interview.

2. Why do you think "Behind the Scenes" is an appropriate title? Create two other titles for this interview.

WEB CONNECTIONS

On the Internet, research other skilled trades. Choose one and create a presentation outlining the knowledge and skills required for the job. Include any information about apprenticeship or training programs that are available in your area.

ANOTHER DAY OF PLANTING IS ALMOST OVER ...

HEY RYAN, HOW MANY YOU UP TO THESE DAYS?

AROUND 800. MAN, MY BACK IS KILLING.

UGHN

DON'T WORRY, YOU'LL –

HEEEEEELP!

OH NO! IT'S MARK!!

HOLD ON, MARK! WE'LL GET YOU OUT OF THERE!

CALL OVER SOME OTHER PLANTERS, LET'S GET THIS GUY OUT!

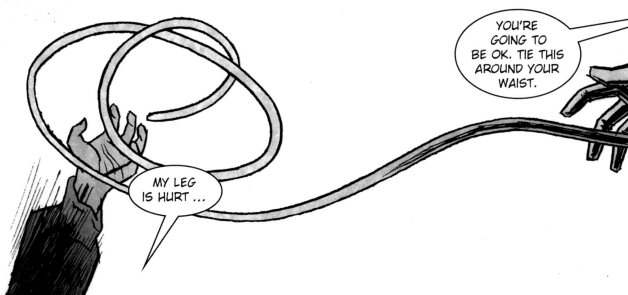

YOU'RE GOING TO BE OK. TIE THIS AROUND YOUR WAIST.

MY LEG IS HURT ...

THANKS, GUYS.

I DON'T THINK I CAN WALK.

DON'T WORRY, I'VE RADIOED THE CAMP. HELP IS ON THE WAY.

THANKS FOR EVERYTHING, GUYS ... IT SUCKS THAT I HAVE TO LEAVE SO SOON. AND JUST WHEN I HAD MADE IT UP TO 1,500 TREES A DAY. YOU'VE GOT MY EMAIL ADDRESS, RIGHT?

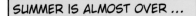

SUMMER IS ALMOST OVER ...

HEY RYAN, I CAN'T BELIEVE YOU'RE AWAKE BEFORE ME THESE DAYS...

I CAN'T BELIEVE IT EITHER. I'M UP TO 1,200 TREES A DAY AND I FEEL GREAT!

WOW! THE FIRST DAY I SAW YOU, I THOUGHT YOU'D END UP LIKE CRAZY EDDIE ...

JUST DON'T LET ME NEAR ANY SHOVELS!

wrap up

Imagine you are Ryan. Write a journal entry about your summer job experience. Share your journal entry with a friend.

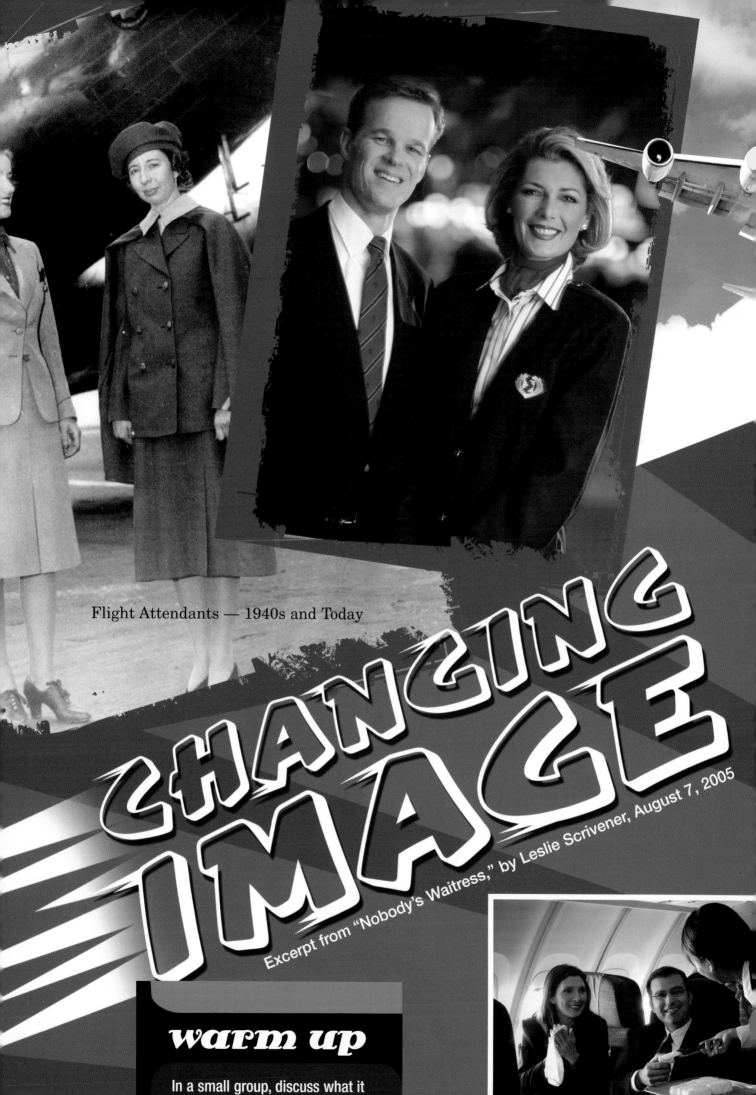

Flight Attendants — 1940s and Today

CHANGING IMAGE

Excerpt from "Nobody's Waitress," by Leslie Scrivener, August 7, 2005

warm up

In a small group, discuss what it takes to be a flight attendant.

CHECKPOINT

Do you agree that the term "stewardesses" used for flight attendants is outdated? Explain your answer.

Don Enns of the Transportation Safety Board summed up their duties last week, even as he called flight attendants by an outdated name: "Stewardesses are not hired as waitresses. They're hired for their safety expertise, and as an aside they serve coffee and dinner." ...

The first flight attendants started working in the U.S. in the 1930s. They were a hardy group, trained as nurses and outfitted in military-style uniforms. They were single and could join the airline only if they were younger than 25, weighed less than 115 pounds, and stood no taller than 5 feet 4 inches. Their duties included hauling luggage, tightening screws on loose seats, and fueling planes.

It's a lovely image — the well-mannered, patient hostess of the skies with buffed nails and upswept hair, offering coffee or tea and checking that seat backs are in the upright position. Nowhere does it mention handcuffing troublesome drunks [or] preparing expectant mothers for emergency delivery at 30,000 feet. ... It definitely doesn't mention getting 297 passengers safely out of a burning plane after a crash landing, as the cabin crew is being praised for doing at Pearson airport last Tuesday.

"... worst case scenarios"

Perhaps safety is a dangerous word for airlines, as it might remind us there's some risk to boarding a plane. It's true that flight attendants spend most of their flying time sorting out the (ever-diminishing) niceties of air travel, and most enjoy and are proud of the service they provide. But they also are expected to spring into action in worst-case scenarios, and as the crash in Air France Flight 358 shows, the worst does happen.

CHECKPOINT

As you read, visualize the changing image of flight attendants.

A few decades later, flying had become a glamour job. The world's most famous fashion houses — Dior, Balenciaga, Pucci — designed airline uniforms in the 1960s and 70s. The bestselling novel *Coffee, Tea or Me?* titillated with stories of beautiful, hard-partying stewardesses jetting between exotic locales. It was an exaggeration, but [France] Pelletier (director of health and safety — for the Canadian airline employees' union) remembers image being paramount in the 1970s. ...

---

niceties: *polite social behaviors*

titillated: *teased*
paramount: *of high importance*

Air France Crash, August 3, 2005

Flight attendants are taught "to say 'Release your seatbelt,' not 'Unfasten,' because they [passengers] might only hear the word 'fasten,'" says Pelletier, who has conducted emergency simulation training. "You see someone frozen, you shout, 'You! Move!' Someone hesitates, you say, 'Go! Go!'"

"We are the last defense..."

Since 9/11, flight attendants have been keenly aware they have added responsibility.

"We are the last defense before you get to the flight deck," says Candace Kolander of the Association of Flight Attendants, the Washington D.C.-based group that represents 46,000 U.S. flight attendants. ...

Flight attendants have been told how to observe passengers, to watch out for nervous-looking ones and the ones who get up from their seats as a group at the same time. They are told to check their food trolleys and look in the galleys for anything unexpected or suspicious.

When Richard Reid tried to ignite a bomb in his shoe aboard an American Airlines flight from Paris in December 2001, it was the flight attendants who stopped him. They had thought his behavior odd — for example, he refused to eat or drink anything on the long flight. Later, they smelled smoke in the cabin and traced it to his seat. When one flight attendant confronted him, she realized he was trying to light his shoe and tried to stop him. In the ensuing scuffle, Reid threw one attendant against a row of seats and bit another before passengers subdued him. ...

[Now] service is what passengers see, what the airlines are selling, and what occupies the bulk of a flight attendant's time. But the unions and many of their members emphasize that they are primarily safety professionals.

Passengers on the Air France plane that crashed at Pearson described the flight attendants moving swiftly into action. One passenger spoke of a flight attendant blanching in fear, but she quickly recovered and was issuing orders to passengers within seconds.

"I was so proud of them when I saw the state of the airplane," says Air Canada purser Bruno Di Giulio. "It could have been catastrophic."

CHECKPOINT
What do you think Bruno Di Guilio means by this?

Such command of the chaos is partly why investigators call the Air France evacuation a "textbook" example of airline safety procedures. In an emergency, passengers have to obey instructions that are often barked out in dark, frightening turmoil.

blanching: *turning pale*
purser: *head flight attendant*

Though men now work as flight attendants, about three-quarters of flight attendants are women.

Job injuries, particularly to the back and neck (from lifting bags to overhead compartments) are common, as are medical problems because of irregular sleeping and eating, working in a pressurized airplane, and coping with unruly passengers.

"I've had people die on flights and people saved on my flights," says one flight attendant. "An elderly woman died on one of my flights and we wrote a letter to her family describing how she had died peacefully in her seat. We wanted her family to know."

wrap up

1. Create a table to show the changes in the job requirements of a flight attendant from the 1930s to the present. Use headings like image, age, responsibilities, and training.

2. Imagine you are a flight attendant on the Air France flight to Toronto. Your first thought after the ordeal is to make sure your family knows that you are safe and unhurt. Write an email to a family member to describe the emergency situation and what you did to get the passengers to safety. Include details, using descriptive words to explain your feelings and experience.

WEB CONNECTIONS

Do an online search for flight attendant jobs on the Internet. Is this a career you would consider for yourself? Why or why not? Compare your answer with a friend's.

Cushy Jobs In SPORTS

Excerpt from *The Toronto Star*, August 7, 2005

warm up

Conduct a survey in class with these questions: What sports do you like? Who is your favorite sports personality? How do you get the latest news about your favorite sport or sports personality?

Trading elbows with Shaquille O'Neal and tackling Jerome Bettis both are major pains, as is managing Manny Ramirez. But every thorn has its rose. And some sports jobs are so dead simple there's ample time to stop and grow the flowers, never mind smell them. Many of the easiest positions are those of backups, out-of-the-spotlight assignments that nonetheless can include unlimited room service and the private number of the local Mercedes dealer. (In the NFL, those are the jobs that CFL players dream about.) Others are full-time occupations, but are so specialized and occasional they require only the infrequent concentration of a Little League outfielder. A look, then, at some of the cushiest jobs in sports:

CHECKPOINT

Scan the headings in this article. How many of these sports jobs are you familiar with? Share what you know with a friend.

Third-String Quarterback

For example: A.J. Feeley, Philadelphia Eagles (2003)

The job: Feeley was pressed into action by the Eagles in 2002 when injuries sidelined starter Donovan MacNabb and backup Koy Detmer. But the 2003 season went smoothly and Feeley put together a perfect stats line — 0 games, 0 pass attempts, 0 completions, 0 yards — while earning $2,892,900.

Perks: Lots of time for dating. …

Toughest task: Coping with clipboard calluses.

Quote: "I have a pretty hefty appetite. I can out-eat my boyfriend."

— *Mitts (Feeley's girlfriend) on how a year of inactivity limits a guy's need for food.*

A.J. Feeley

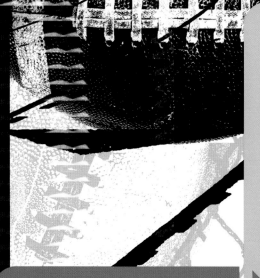

Punter

For example: Hunter Smith, Indianapolis Colts

The job: Punters are considered necessary evils, but even so, Tom Oates of the Madison-based *Wisconsin State Journal* was agog when Green Bay Packers coach Mike Sherman opted to keep two punters — Bryan Barker and B.J. Sander — on his 53-man roster last fall. "Keeping two punters is the equivalent of keeping two sand wedges in your golf bag," Oates wrote. "If you're good, you don't even have that much use for one of them."

Perks: In Smith's case, a six-year, $4.78 million contract.

Toughest task: Looking busy when the coaches bring out the tackling dummies.

Quote: "That's life as a punter. You're known for holds, or a fake field goal or not punting. It's a very eccentric position on the field."

— *Smith, after two consecutive playoff games without a single punt.*

agog: *excited*
eccentric: *odd*

CHECKPOINT

Notice that "Toughest task" is written tongue-in-cheek and is not meant to be taken seriously. Think of what it really takes for each sports personality to earn his keep.

Backup Goalie (Hockey)

For example: Ron Tugnutt, Dallas Stars

The job: Used to be that a back-up NHL goalie's primary responsibility was to shop for leg pads … Beyond equipment planning, it is occasionally necessary to play, usually against teams that would struggle in the AHL or that have Phil Esposito as an executive.

Perks: Tugnutt was paid $2.8 million in 2003-04 for appearing in 11 games — four of those thanks to a suspension to starter Marty Turco, who nonetheless played in 73 games that season. Tugnutt spent 547 minutes and 38 seconds in net, meaning he made $306,770 per hour of playing time.

Toughest task: Just saying no when teammates pass around the ammonia capsules — the respiratory stimulant can make it hard to doze.

Quote: "I want to get some games, help out the team, help out Marty. I want to basically come and do what I was brought here to do in the first place."

— *Tugnutt on returning from injury, whereupon his teammates said: "Sorry, were you away?"*

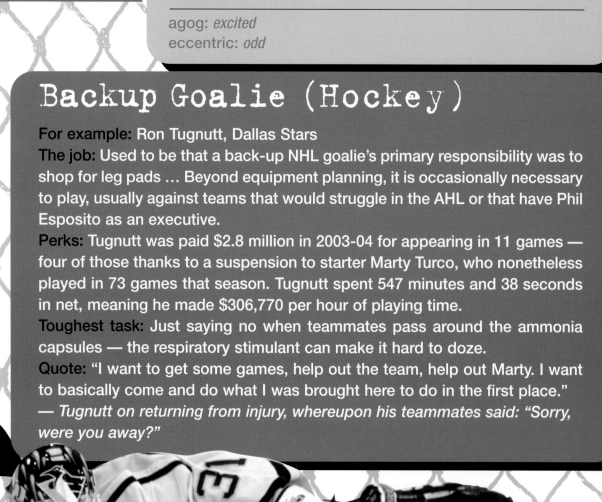

Ron Tugnutt

Situational Left-Hander

For example: John Franco

The job: In the month of April this year, the 44-year-old Franco pitched a grand total of three innings for the Houston Astros, throwing 54 pitches. Fifty-four pitches. There are starters who throw more in the bullpen as a warm-up. Mind you, there's a price to be paid for such inactivity. In July the Astros decided his contribution was so minimal (7.20 ERA) they cut him. He continues to collect his $700,000 salary, however.

Perks: Free sunflower seeds.

Toughest task: Finding floss in the clubhouse to dislodge sunflower seeds.

Quote: "There's a lot of guys doing it (who are) younger than me."
— *Franco, on not being embarrassed at his specialized, late-career role.*

NHL Goal Judge

For example: Dave Keon Jr.

The job: The pay and travel are not as lavish as other cushy sports jobs, but, on the plus side, there's a near-total lack of responsibility. You sit in a small booth with a spectacular, behind-the-net view of the game and occasionally press a button to turn on a red light. If you hit the button at the wrong time there are zero ramifications. Not only can the referee overrule you, the NHL also has video replay judges. The position has become ceremonial and anachronistic like, say, the Queen.

Perks: Front-row seats.

Toughest task: Holding it in while waiting for the end-of-period bathroom breaks.

Quote: "The goalie did the splits and I never saw it after that."
— *Goal judge Paul McInnis describes missing a goal in the 2003 playoffs.*

---

ramifications: *effects*
anachronistic: *out of date*

John Franco

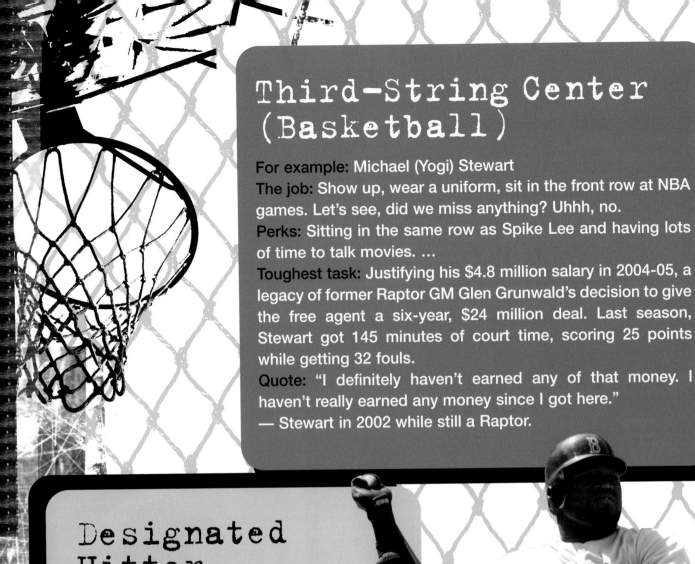

Third-String Center (Basketball)

For example: Michael (Yogi) Stewart
The job: Show up, wear a uniform, sit in the front row at NBA games. Let's see, did we miss anything? Uhhh, no.
Perks: Sitting in the same row as Spike Lee and having lots of time to talk movies. ...
Toughest task: Justifying his $4.8 million salary in 2004-05, a legacy of former Raptor GM Glen Grunwald's decision to give the free agent a six-year, $24 million deal. Last season, Stewart got 145 minutes of court time, scoring 25 points while getting 32 fouls.
Quote: "I definitely haven't earned any of that money. I haven't really earned any money since I got here."
— Stewart in 2002 while still a Raptor.

Designated Hitter

For example: David Ortiz, Boston Red Sox
The job: Swinging the bat approximately 10 times during a three-hour baseball game — less if you're patient or replaced by a pinch-hitter. Occasionally laughing at the knee-weary catchers, who are required to pop up and down like hyperactive gophers.
Perks: Lots of time to watch Curt Schilling lose on Celebrity Poker in the clubhouse.
Toughest task: A tie: Pretending that workouts are even remotely necessary to do your job and not getting tired of leading the "Hey fans in the stands, if you're with us clap your hands" cheers.
Quote: "The DH is the easiest job in baseball, except for maybe being a starting pitcher."
— The Colorado Rockies' Dante Bichette, doing some serious dissing after his first DH experience.

David Ortiz

Backup Goalie (Soccer)

For example: Carlo Cudicini, Chelsea

The job: Alan Smith of the Daily Telegraph suggested in 2002 that fullback was the easiest job in soccer. "Know what you are doing and you can play there 'til you're 40. Make a few tackles, knock it up the line. What could be simpler?" he wrote. Well, not playing, for one thing. Cudicini appeared in only 11 games for the richest team in soccer last season — about 1 a month — only three of which were Premier League contests and all those came after Chelsea had clinched the league championship. Cudicini managed to reduce his workload further by getting red-carded in one game and being replaced in another.

Perks: Paychecks signed by billionaire Roman Abramovich.

Toughest task: Slicing the oranges.

Quote: "Carlo ... has done as much work as me all season, it is just that I have played the games."

— Chelsea No.1 keeper Petr Cech unwittingly insults Cudicini with faint praise.

Chelsea: *soccer team in London, England*

unwittingly: *without knowing*

wrap up

1. With a partner, pick 10 sports terms or expressions from this article and create a glossary for non-sports fans. Combine your work with other groups in class to create a master list for display.

2. Imagine you are holding one of the cushy jobs mentioned in the article. Write a journal entry to describe an eventful day on the job, and what it means to you.

WEB CONNECTIONS

Use the Internet to gather information you need to create a poster for any one of the sports jobs mentioned in the article. State what the job is, and include a description of work responsibilities, required skills and abilities, pay, and benefits.

Carlo Cudicini

THE
PROFESSIONAL

By Kenneth L. Shipley

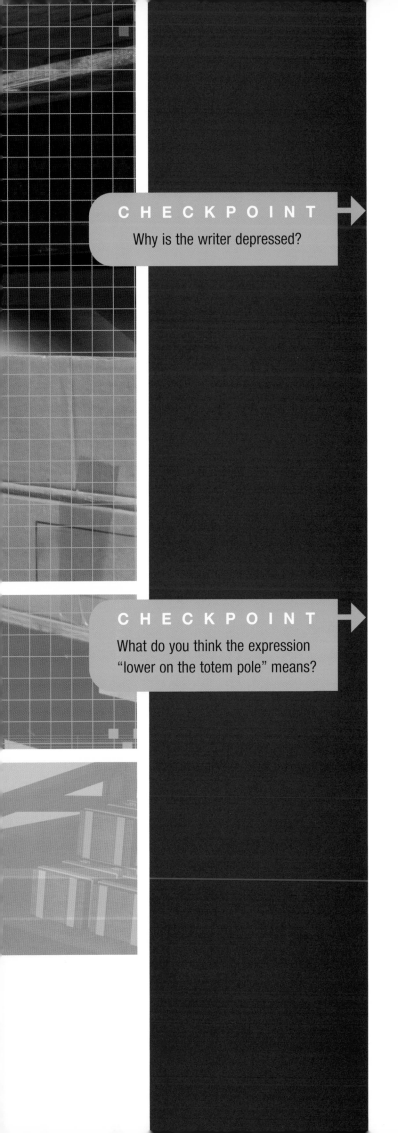

CHECKPOINT →

Why is the writer depressed?

CHECKPOINT →

What do you think the expression "lower on the totem pole" means?

I went to the dark end of the inventory shelves, pressed my forehead against the wall and indulged myself in a few moments of quiet despair. Was this the way it would be for the rest of my life? Here I was, two years out of school, working at yet another mindless, low-paying, dead-end job. Up to this point, I had avoided the question by just not thinking about it, but now, for some reason, I could not. The thought sucked every bit of energy from my body. I clocked out sick, went home to bed, pulled the covers over my head, and tried to forget about tomorrow and all the tomorrows that would follow.

By morning I was a little more composed, but no less depressed. Listlessly, I went back to work and resumed my hopeless drudgery.

There were several new guys on the job that morning — temporary workers even lower on the totem pole than I was. One of them caught my eye. He was older than the others, and wearing a uniform. The company didn't issue uniforms — in fact, the company didn't care what you wore as long as you showed up. But this guy was decked out in smartly pressed tan trousers and work shirt, complete with his name, Jim, embroidered on the pocket. I guess he supplied himself with the uniform.

I watched him all that day and the rest of the days he worked with us. He was never late or early. He worked at a steady, unhurried pace. He was friendly to everyone he worked with, but rarely talked while he was working. He took the

Listlessly: *without energy*

designated breaks at midmorning and afternoon with everyone else, but unlike many others, he never lingered past the allotted time.

Some of the crew brown-bagged lunch, but most of us got our meals and drinks from the vending machines. Jim didn't do either. He ate his lunch from an old-fashioned steel lunch box and drank his coffee from a Thermos bottle — both of them well-worn with use. Sometimes people would be a little careless about cleaning up after they ate. Jim's place at the table was spotless, and, of course, he was always back on the line exactly on time. He wasn't just odd, he was outstanding — admirable!

He was the kind of worker managers dream of. Despite that, the other workers liked him, too. He didn't try to show anybody up. He did what was asked of him, no more, no less. He didn't gossip or complain or argue. He just did the job — common labor — with more personal dignity than I had believed was possible with this kind of low-level, grunt work.

designated: *specified*

CHECKPOINT
Pick out the details that show Jim to be a professional.

His attitude and every action proclaimed that he was a professional. Labor might be common; he wasn't.

When the temporary work was finished, Jim left for another job, but the impression he made on me didn't. Even though I had never talked to him, he turned my head completely around. I did the best I could to follow his example.

I didn't buy a lunch box or a uniform, but I did start setting my own standards. I worked like a businessman fulfilling a contract, just the way Jim had done. To my great surprise, the managers noticed my new productivity and promoted me. A few years later, I promoted myself to a better-paying job with a different company. And so it went. Eventually, many companies and many years later, I started a business of my own.

Whatever success I've had has been the result of hard work and good luck, but I think the biggest part of my luck was the lesson I learned from Jim so long ago. Respect doesn't come from the kind of work you do; it comes from the way you do the work.

CHECKPOINT
Note Jim's influence on the writer.

wrap up

1. Using ideas from the article, create a chart with two columns. In the first column list all items beginning with **Do** (e.g., Do be punctual). In the second column list all items beginning with **Don't** (e.g., Don't gossip at work).

2. With a partner, role-play a conversation between Jim and the writer when they meet many years later. What will the writer say to express his appreciation for the lesson learned? What will Jim say?

WEB CONNECTIONS

Use the Internet to research factory jobs. Read a news article on the topic and summarize what you read to share with the class.

GET ME SOME *Poet*

Christopher Dreher, *Globe and Mail*, June 18, 2005

In his new book, *A Whole New Mind: Moving from the Information Age to the Conceptual Age*, Mr. [Daniel] Pink argues that the North American white-collar employment scene is tilting in favor of fields that often have been considered secondary, even frivolous. Jobs that demand rational, bottom-line-oriented skills are endangered. Business graduates could replace English majors as the ones stuck living in their parents' basements.

"To some people, this might sound like wishful thinking," Mr. Pink says. "Wouldn't it be wonderful if we moved toward valuing artistic work more, or something like that?" ...

FYI

The Information Age is characterized by computer technology and the availability of information. The emphasis is on speed and logical and precise ways of thinking. In the Conceptual Age, artistry, empathy, and emotion will come into play.

Mr. Pink contends that in the West, the Information Age is giving way to a "Conceptual Age." He points to three developments that are undermining the importance of number crunching and technical skills — call them the three A's.

The first is abundance. In a society where goods are cheap and plentiful, a product's value is not just in its function but in its style or uniqueness. ...

CHECKPOINT

What images come to mind when you think about automation in the workplace?

The other two A-factors are more familiar — automation and Asia.

But Mr. Pink is not rehashing the now-familiar fate of blue-collar workers whose factory jobs have gone to a developing nation. He's talking about a similar shift in the white-collar economy, which is seeing a large swath of tasks moving to educated but much-lower waged professionals in poor countries.

Computer-programming chores, for instance, are now routinely passed to Indian workers, whom the Internet has made as convenient to hire as a programmer who drives in from the suburbs. A similar pattern of outsourcing rote duties is appearing in law, medicine, and publishing.

Meanwhile, tasks that used to require a high-level professional are being automated with powerful new software, or accomplished by clients themselves on the Internet. Tax preparation, divorce agreements and business contracts, and even medical procedures such as reading charts can now be done quickly and cheaply online. ...

But along with the jobs that vanish, new roles will appear to provide added value in the global marketplace. "In a world enriched by abundance but disrupted by the automation and outsourcing of white-collar work," Mr. Pink writes, "everyone regardless of profession must cultivate an artistic sensibility. We may not all be Dali or Degas. But today we must all be designers."

CHECKPOINT

Do you agree with this statement? Think of reasons to support your opinion.

---

rehashing: *repeating*
swath: *chunk, volume*

outsourcing: *sending work to an outside provider*
rote: *routine*

He points to a London Business School study claiming that for every percentage point of profit that is invested in product design, a company's sales and profits rise by an average of three to four percent. The number of graphic designers in the United States has increased tenfold over the past decade. Now "graphic designers outnumber chemical engineers by four to one."

CHECKPOINT

Other than design and appearance, what else would you consider when buying a new gadget?

Consider the iPod. Though no more powerful than many MP3 players, it dominates with its sleek look and interactive design. ...

Mr. Pink cites business leaders who have voiced appreciation for this change. "Get me some poets as managers. Poets are our original systems thinkers," said Sidney Harman, CEO of a multimillion-dollar stereo-equipment empire.

When asked how his reign as head of General Motors would differ from his predecessor's, salty former marine Robert Lutz said, "I see us being in the art business. Art, entertainment, and mobile sculpture, which, coincidentally, also happens to provide transportation."

Likewise, BMW executive Chris Bangle has said, "We don't make 'automobiles.' BMW makes moving works of art that express the driver's love of quality."...

wrap up

1. Using your own words, describe what Mr. Pink means by the three A's.

2. If business leaders agree with Mr. Pink's ideas about the new Conceptual Age, what kinds of careers and jobs will be in demand? Brainstorm with a partner and create a list to share with the class.

WEB CONNECTIONS

Do you think it is a good idea to outsource work? In a small group, discuss the pros and cons of this business practice and present your views in a short report. Include statistics and information from the Internet to support your position.

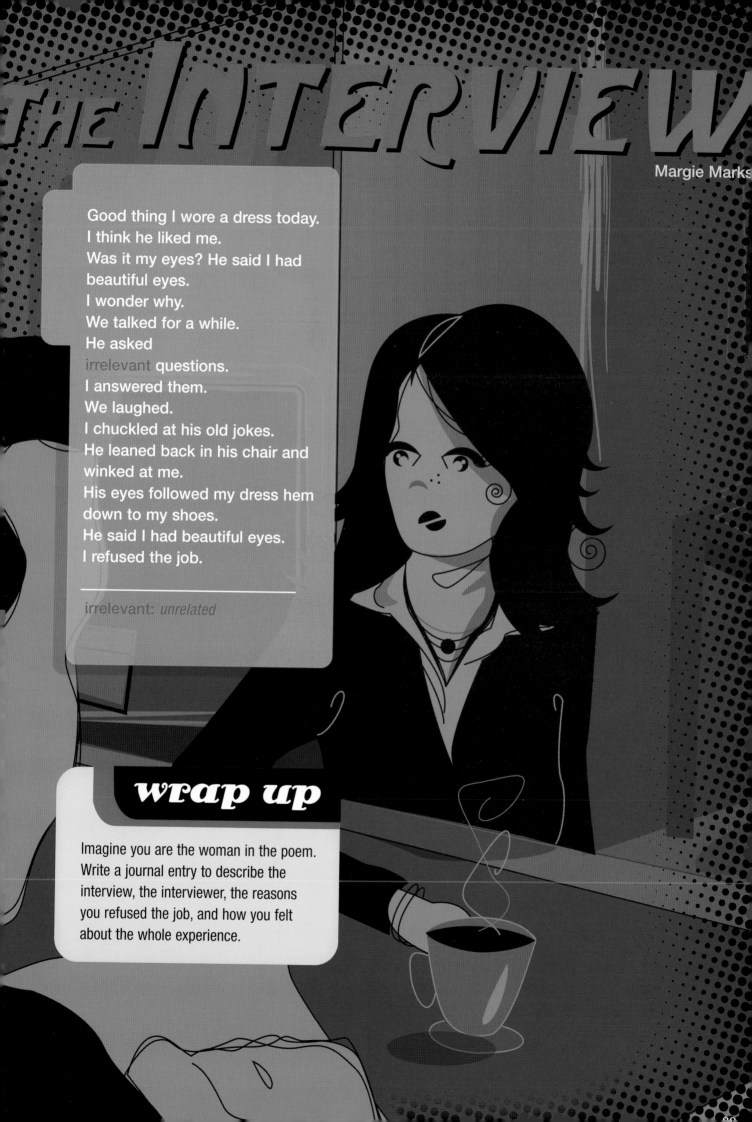

THE INTERVIEW

Margie Marks

Good thing I wore a dress today.
I think he liked me.
Was it my eyes? He said I had
beautiful eyes.
I wonder why.
We talked for a while.
He asked
irrelevant questions.
I answered them.
We laughed.
I chuckled at his old jokes.
He leaned back in his chair and
winked at me.
His eyes followed my dress hem
down to my shoes.
He said I had beautiful eyes.
I refused the job.

_____

irrelevant: *unrelated*

wrap up

Imagine you are the woman in the poem.
Write a journal entry to describe the
interview, the interviewer, the reasons
you refused the job, and how you felt
about the whole experience.

DEAR ALEX ...

warm up

Do you think writing to someone you do not know for advice is a good idea? What are some reasons for and against doing it?

Traditionally, the Advice Column appears as a feature in newspapers and magazines. It allows the readers to express their concerns and get feedback, usually from experts in the field. The following letters to Alex highlight workplace issues.

Dear Alex,

I was very happy in my job until last month when I was transferred to a new department. Now I work with a supervisor who's quite different from the ones I have worked with before. He is new in the company but he acts as if he knows everything. He bosses me around, gives me more work than I can handle, and expects me to work late. I'm thinking of quitting, but I really don't want to start all over at a new job, probably with lower pay. What should I do?

— Miserable

Dear Miserable,

I understand that you are unhappy but try not to make any rash decisions. Your supervisor is new on the job and this might explain why things are so hectic now. If you can't work late or meet an impossible deadline, it's best to talk to him. Ask for his advice about reorganizing your workload. Give yourself a little more time — things may change.

— Alex

Dear Alex,

I work with a bunch of people who are always complaining. When we are together during breaks or at lunch, all they do is gossip about others, say nasty things about the boss, or whine about work. I don't enjoy these conversations, but these people are on my project team and we are always together. Should I make excuses and stay away?

— Disturbed

Dear Disturbed,

Staying away may not be the best solution. These are people you work with and you want to get along with them. Looking at the bright side, the workplace is where you get to meet all kinds of people and perhaps make friends. If you hear things that are not true or you don't agree with, it's okay to say it. You could even change the topic. Who knows — they may even stop whining and gossiping when they realize it is not helping.

— Alex

Dear Alex,

I am very grateful to my present manager whose strong recommendation got me my present position three months ago. She has also devoted much time to training me on the job. Now a competing company has offered me better pay to do the same work, with the promise of promotion in six months. Should I take the offer and walk out on my manager? I don't want to appear ungrateful and let my manager down after what she has done for me. What should I do?

— Feeling Disloyal

Dear Feeling Disloyal,

Making a career move is a difficult decision for anyone! It's natural to feel guilty, especially when you think you are abandoning someone who has treated you well. But you have to do what is best for yourself and your career. Your manager will consider your decision to leave as a loss, but she'll want what's best for you. And you can continue to stay in touch with her!

— Alex

wrap up

1. Pick one of the above letters and write your own response. Offer advice that will help make the writer feel better. Read your letter to the class.

2. Imagine you are "Feeling Disloyal" in the third situation. Role-play a conversation between you and your manager when you tell her about your decision to quit.

WEB CONNECTIONS

Today, many people create their own blogs (online journals) where they share opinions on a whole range of matters. Search the Internet for blogging on the job. Summarize some main points about employee blogging.

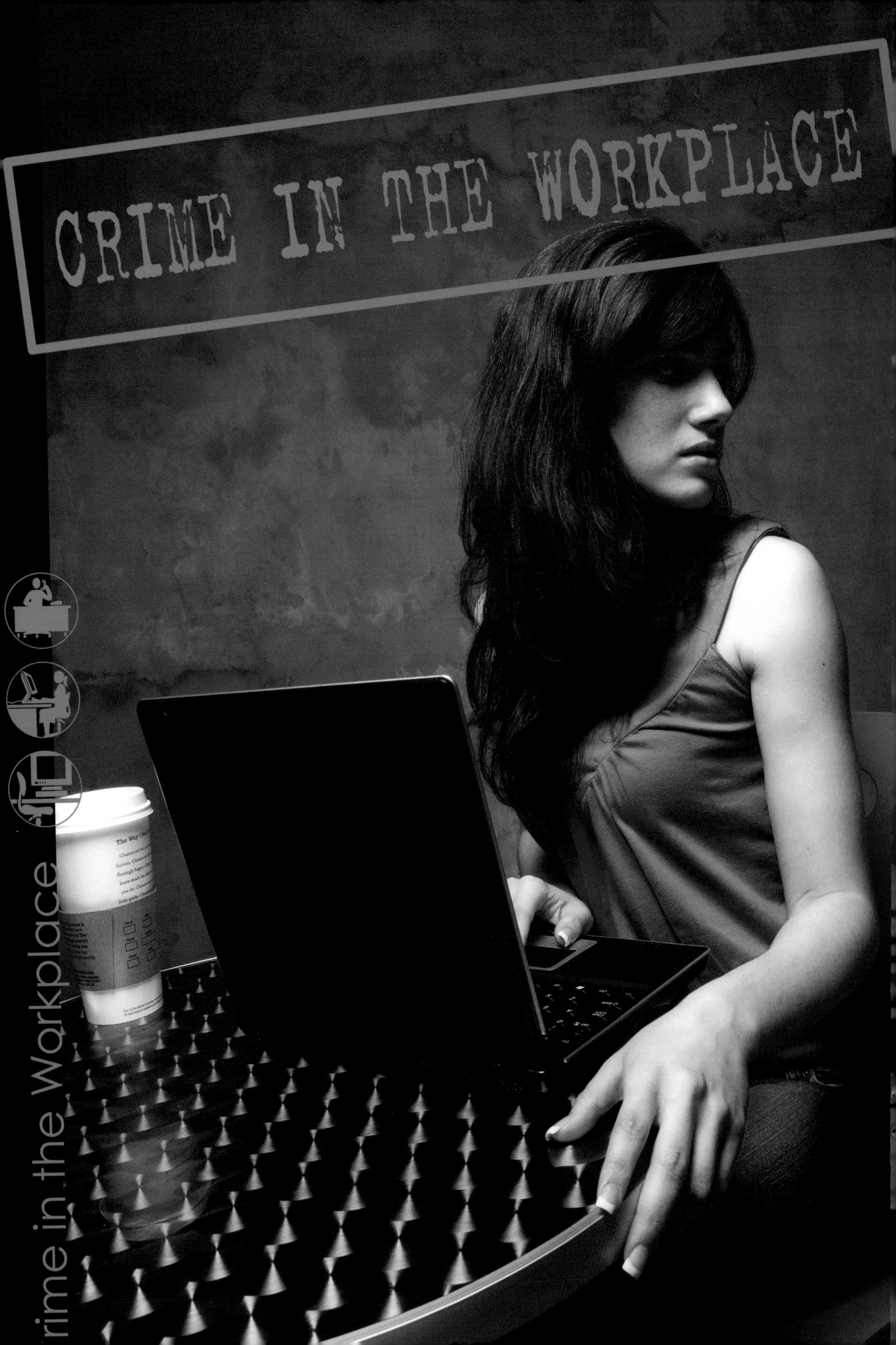
CRIME IN THE WORKPLACE
rime in the Workplace

Sam Ayala   Mr. Dalton   Steve Murphy   Police Officer   Neighbor   Detective Bennett

warm up

In a group, brainstorm examples of workplace crimes. Share stories that you have heard or read about in the newspapers.

Scene 1: Office of a computer firm

Narrator: Sam Ayala is an accounts assistant at a small computer company. It's 7:00 PM — and he has promised to take his wife to a movie tonight. He's determined to keep his promise.

CHECKPOINT
As you read, pick out clues to show that Sam is overworked.

Sam: [Rushing toward the door] Phew! This work pace is no joke. Checking orders, invoicing, coordinating incoming and outgoing shipments and collections, and answering endless inquiries – everything is urgent. I really need a vacation.

Narrator: The door opens and Sam's boss Mr. Dalton enters.

Mr. Dalton: Just the person I wanted! Listen, Sam, get hold of King Distributors first thing tomorrow. I'm counting on the payment for the memory chips we shipped 10 days ago. That's $30,000 we're waiting for!

Sam: No problem, sir. I'll take care of it first thing tomorrow. Goodnight.

Mr. Dalton: Goodnight, Sam.

Scene 2: The next morning. Sam is on the phone with Steve — accountant at King Distributors. Mr. Dalton is at another larger desk.

Sam: Hi Steve, do me a favor. Please rush out the check for the memory chips we shipped to you. King Distributors has never been late before.

Steve: What shipment? We're still waiting for the memory chips! I was about to call you. What's the matter? Short-handed?

Sam: Of course not. Listen, Steve, I have to go now. I'll get back to you within the hour.

Narrator: Sam frantically looks through his computer records.

Sam: Hey, here it is — an order from King Distributors, a shipment to King's warehouse address at 1500 Elm Street, and the name of the shipping agent. I'll let Steve know about this.

Narrator: Sam phones Steve again.

Sam: Hi Steve, about that shipment of chips — I've got the shipment date, agent's confirmation, and receipt from your 1500 Elm Street warehouse. The chips are packed tightly. It's only a small parcel. Perhaps someone overlooked the package.

Steve: Sam, did you say 1500 Elm Street? Our warehouse is at 150 Elm Street!

Narrator: Sam is now worried. He double-checks his computer record. The address on file is 1500 Elm Street. Then he walks to Mr. Dalton's office.

Sam: Mr. Dalton, did King relocate and not inform us?

Mr. Dalton: Ask Shirley. She ought to know, she's the sales rep.

Sam: Shirley's away on vacation, but I have her cell phone number. I'll talk to her.

Mr. Dalton: Don't stop at that. Get over to King's. That parcel could be sitting in someone's warehouse. Put aside your other work. $30,000 is more important!

Narrator: Sam leaves a phone message for Shirley.

Sam: Hi Shirley — been trying to get hold of you. About the King Distributors computer chips — do you know anything about the mix-up? If you get this

CHECKPOINT

What makes Sam think that something is wrong?

message, give me a call on my cell. I'm going to check out 1500 Elm Street.

Scene 3: Sam is standing in front of a modest home. He's on his cell with Mr. Dalton.

Sam: Mr. Dalton. It's Sam. I went to 1500 Elm Street. It's nothing but an empty warehouse. {Pause} Yes sir. I know — very serious. {Pause} Yes sir, I'm at Shirley's house now. Maybe she can make sense of this.

Narrator: Sam climbs the steps to the porch and knocks loudly several times on the door.

Sam: Guess she is out of town.

Narrator: A neighbor approaches.

Neighbor: Is Shirley all right? She moved out last week without saying goodbye or leaving a forwarding address. Mail has been piling up.

Sam: Something's terribly wrong. Excuse me. I have to call my boss.

Narrator: Sam is on the phone with Mr. Dalton again.

Sam: Mr. Dalton? Sam again. It doesn't look good, sir. Do you think Shirley is behind the missing chips?

Mr. Dalton: I think Shirley is involved. We've got to call the police.

Narrator: The neighbor leaves after talking with Sam. A police officer and Mr. Dalton show up. The officer takes notes as she questions Sam and Mr. Dalton.

Mr. Dalton: Shirley's been with this company for ten years now. A good worker and a team player. I like her. I certainly consider her trustworthy.

Sam: Shirley works every hard. She's friendly and gets along with everyone. She's the one who got me an interview for this job.

Officer: Has anything changed recently?

Sam: Not her work. But lately we've joked about how she looks like a million bucks – really expensive clothes, make-up, and fine jewelry.

Mr. Dalton: Sam's right. Shirley looks different these days. Some staff commented on the number of outfits she

owns. They said someone must have given her a lot of money.

Sam: Shirley's a friend. She helped me a lot when I first joined the company, especially on the computer. She's so good at it.

Officer: Well, it seems like someone has altered King's address on the computer. Can I assume that a personal ID and password are required to get into the records?

Mr. Dalton: Yes, Officer. And we are very careful about security. Sam and I are the only two people in the office who can access client records.

> ### CHECKPOINT
> Note what Mr. Dalton says about information security in his office.

Sam: Oh no! I once told Shirley my ID and password. But that was a long time ago when she was showing me how to use the customer database program.

Officer: There is enough information for an investigation. I'll file a report and someone will get back to you.

Scene 4: Mr. Dalton and Sam are in the office. A plainclothes detective enters.

Detective: Mr. Dalton? Mr. Ayala? I'm Detective Rob Bennett.

Mr. Dalton: Good to see you, sir. What can you tell us about our missing computer chips?

Detective: Our investigation revealed that King's address in your company's database was indeed altered a few days before the shipment. We found out that

Shirley Gallagher accessed the company's database using Sam's ID and password. The janitor recalled having seen Shirley alone at Sam's computer very late one night.

Sam: But, why?

Detective: Shirley has a lot of unpaid bills for clothes and jewelry. She is deep in debt.

Mr. Dalton: Oh no!

Detective: We have Shirley in custody now. She confessed to changing the database and using the fake address to receive the shipment.

Mr. Dalton: I can't imagine a trusted long-time employee doing that.

Detective: You'd be surprised by the number of such crimes.

wrap up

1. Imagine you are Sam and you are asked to write a report for the police. In a paragraph, describe what happened and what you found out. Stick to the facts of the story.

2. Work with a partner to create a script of the conversation between Shirley and the police officer that leads to her confession. Role-play your script for the class.

WEB CONNECTIONS

Using the Internet, key in the search words workplace crime prevention. Pick out one example of workplace crime and make a list of prevention measures. Share your list with a partner.

ACKNOWLEDGMENTS

The publisher gratefully acknowledges the following for permission to reprint copyrighted material in this book.

Every reasonable effort has been made to trace the owners of copyrighted material and to make due acknowledgment. Any errors or omissions drawn to our attention will be gladly rectified in future editions.

Kenneth L. Shipley: "The Professional." *Chicken Soup for the Soul at Work*. Permission courtesy of Kenneth L. Shipley.

Leslie Scrivener: "Nobody's Waitress." *The Toronto Star*. Reprinted with permission — Torstar Syndication Services.

Christopher Dreher: "Get Me Some Poets as Managers." *The Globe and Mail*. Permission courtesy of Christopher Dreher.

"Pilot Loves Working in Algonquin." *Metro*. Reprinted with permission — Torstar Syndication Services.

"Profile: Ann Schuessler." *Seattle Daily Journal of Commerce*. Permission courtesy of Seattle Daily Journal.

"Cushy Jobs in Sports." *The Toronto Star*. Reprinted with permission — Torstar Syndication Services.